'n

Calico

POETRY OF THE WEST

For Bill,
 It is nice to meet someone who shares my love for poetry. Keep writing — and find your poet's voice. Best Wishes!
 Ann Sorkat

Cowhide 'n Calico

A POET LOOKS AT THE WEST

By
Ann Sochat & Tony Cano

Reata Publishing • Canutillo, Texas

Copyright © 1997
Reata Publishing Company

Cowhide 'n Calico
A Poet Looks at the West

All rights reserved under international and Pan-American Copyright conventions. This book may not be reproduced in whole or in part by any form or by any media without written permission from Reata Publishing Company, except in the case of brief quotations embodied in critical essays or reviews.

ISBN 0-9639210-3-7

Library of Congress
Catalog Card Number: 96-092891

First Printing, January 1997

Printed in the United States of America by Reata Publishing Company, 120-A La Nell Street, Canutillo, Texas 79835

All inquiries for purchases of this book should be addressed to Reata Publishing Company. Fax inquiries may be made by faxing 915-877-4485.

DEDICATION

For the brothers and sisters everywhere, who share not only our genes and our memories, but who share our triumphs and our sorrows with an open heart...for Linden and Joe.

Books By
Ann Sochat & Tony Cano

Dutch Oven Cooking with Tony Cano

Echoes in the Wind
Ranch Recollections and Poetry

Chuck Wagon Heyday
The History & Color of the Chuck Wagon at Work

Cowhide 'n Calico
A Poet Looks at the West

Bandido
The True Story of Chico Cano, the Last Western Bandit
(Coming in April, 1997)

ABOUT THE AUTHORS

Ann Sochat wrote the text and poetry for *Cowhide 'n Calico*. She performs in Western and cowboy symposiums, and her poems have been published in *Western Horseman* magazines and their 1996 and 1997 Buying Guides. Her work reflects the love and respect she has for the men and women who settled the West and are still found ranching it today.

Tony Cano developed the technical design for the book and was involved in its editing and production. An authority on Western trail drives and roundups, he attends cowboy symposiums with Ms. Sochat where they speak about Western-related topics and do seminars on Dutch oven cooking. Both authors are members of Western Writers of America, Texas Cowboy Poets Association, Academy of Performing Artists, and the Western History Association.

TABLE OF CONTENTS

RANCHING FAMILIES	11
Introduction	12
Ranchin' Family	13
Genes	15
Roy 'n Gene	17
Western Women	20
Grandma	23
Lessons Tooled in Leather	25
GROWING UP ON A RANCH	29
Introduction	30
An' How I'd Ride	31
The Old Schoolhouse	35
Cowboy Lullaby	37
COWBOYS AND LOVE	39
Introduction	40
Dude Boots	41
A Cowboy's Love	46
ABC's of Cowboys	48
ON THE TRAIL	51
Introduction	52
RoundupTime	53
Line-camp Christmas	55
Chuckwagon Charlie	57

MAIL	59
Introduction	60
Lock of Hair	61
Mail-order Memories	65
HORSES	67
Introduction	68
My Best Pal	69
Wild Horses	72
COWBOY CODE	73
Introduction	74
Code of the Cowboy	75
A Cowboy's Thanks	77
THE CHANGING WEST	79
Introduction	80
Entrepeneur	81
Why?	85
Good Ol' Days	87
END OF THE TRAIL	89
Introduction	90
Sunset	91
Treasure	94
Immortality	96

The Ranching Family

There was a strong sense of the extended family to be found on the ranches of the West. Children grew up on land their parents had cleared or fenced or claimed, to marry and continue with the tradition, for to own land was to have roots and worth. The elders helped care for the young, until the circle reversed and the young were old enough to care for the elders.

A Ranchin' Family

I guess the thing my folks was best at
Was child procreation,
And each birth of son or daughter
Was a cause for celebration!
And Pa would always tease my ma
When she became distraught,
"We won't need to hire ranch hands
With this healthy crew we've got!"

And we grew up a rowdy bunch
Full of fun an' full of laughter.
There was always someone runnin',
And someone chasin' after!
And there were children everywhere,
In the barn and in the stable,
And we played like pups out on the loose,
And we fought like Cain an' Abel!

And we all pitched in to do the chores;
There were lots of hands for work.
Though it sometimes took remindin',
Pa would whup the kid who'd shirk!
For that time, I guess my folks
Were pretty liberal in their standin'.
The boys helped in the kitchen;
The girls helped to do the brandin'.

When we came out a-whoopin'
After the chores were done,
All the goats an' all the chickens
Would sure scatter on the run!
And when we went out ridin',
You could hear us miles away.
"Guess the Bar-S kids are blowin' steam!"
The folks around would say.

And we learned respect for livin' things,
And to take care of the land,
And that we were all just one small part
Of the world that God had planned!
As grownups, when we gather now,
It is somethin' grand to see.
We're a close-knit, boisterous, sharin',
Lovin', ranchin' family!

And my pa's favorite sayin' is,
"I raised my livestock PRIME!
He'll tell us, "I've raised cows an' pigs
An' horses in my time.
But of all the things I've raised in life,
I will brag, if I'm allowed,
Of the finest herd of boys an' girls.
You have really done me proud!"

Genes

I was just a child on my parents' ranch
When they sat me on a horse,
So learning to handle a cowboy's chores
Was just a matter of course.
I'd cry when I got left behind;
I wanted to ride with the boys.
No dolls or tea sets, I'd follow my brothers,
If given any choice.
And they were pretty tough on me,
Not cuttin' me any slack,
I knew that if I cried or complained,
That they would send me back.
And I'd spend all day in the saddle,
Bringin' up the rear,
I'd do all sorts of menial jobs
If they'd let me just stay near.
In my mom and dad's discussions,
She'd say to him teasingly,
"Her toughness comes from YOUR family;
She got her looks from me!"

As I grew older, my mother tried
To make me more refined,
But to my rough and tumble ways
She soon became resigned.
I was as good a hand as any boy,
An' I'd fight to prove my point.
I wouldn't give in, no matter whose nose
I pushed out of joint.
I took the teasing they dished out;
I gave some back in turn.
I knew that their respect was something

I would have to earn.
I no longer followed my brothers;
I clearly led the way.
As my parents would be talking,
I'd hear my mother say,
"That need to always win, my dear,
I think you will agree,
Comes directly from YOUR family;
She got her looks from me!"

My brothers all got older;
One by one, they moved away.
Of the children on the ranch,
I was the only one to stay.
Then came the fall my dad got hurt
And had to stay in bed.
Frustration mixed with pain
As he tried hard to lift his head.
"What about the balin'?"
"Done!" Mom said.
"What about the fences?"   "Fixed!"
"What about the cattle?"   "Safe!" she said,
With pride and annoyance mixed.
"Your daughter and I took care of things;
We really had no choice."
And I heard that pride re-echoed
In my father's shaky voice,
"You know, my dear, you must admit,
Now it's clear for all to see:
Her strength comes from YOUR family;
She got her looks from ME!"

Roy 'n Gene

When I was young, the biggest treat
Was when we'd get to go
On Saturday afternoon to town
To see a picture show.
It was a real small theater.
They charged but a small price,
An' they didn't mind if we stayed around
And watched the movie twice.
Our world was centered round the action
On that silver screen,
As we watched our favorite heroes,
The cowboys Roy an' Gene.

As Pa would drive us home from town,
We couldn't wait to play,
An' recreate the scenes we'd seen
Upon the screen that day,
But when we reached the ranch,
There were always chores to do.
Ma said, "No playin' cowboys
Until you all are through!"
So we helped her with the milking,
Put the livestock in their pens,
An' we had to put out evening feed
For the horses an' the hens.
But then we'd grab our cap guns
An' head for the ravine,
Where we'd take turns at bein'
Our heroes Roy an' Gene.

Or we'd run down by the bunkhouse,
A favorite place to play,
Where the ranchhands were resting
From working hard all day.
We'd help them as they cleaned
Their leather tack with saddle soap,
An' sometimes they would take the time
To teach us how to rope.
An' when we said, "REAL cowboys
Is what we want to be."
They'd widely grin or slap their legs
An' laugh at my brother an' me.
But sure, we didn't mind it,
Because we had a dream:
We'd grow up to be cowboys,
Just like Roy an' Gene.

It took years of livin' at the ranch
To open up our eyes.
Diggin' fence posts, mendin' wire,
Hard work made us realize,
That throughout all of the trying times
Our family had to weather,
It was the courage of my Ma an' Pa
That kept our ranch together.
An' cowboyin' ain't bout
Chasin' outlaws with a gun,
But it's working hard with no reward
Except for a job well done.
Those cowboy movies should have been more honest,

Like I figger,
They should have had Roy shovelin'
Behind that horse named Trigger!
An' though they shore ain't famous
An' they ain't quick on the draw,
The REAL cowboy heroes
Are just plain men like my Pa.
They ain't the dashin' figures
That you see up on the screen.
Some things you learn as you grow up!
Sorry, Roy an' Gene!

Western Women

My Mom had stayed out on the ranch,
It was her cannin' day.
She'd said, "This fruit is ripe
An' must be put up right away!
By the time you all get back from town,
I should be almost done.
Now, you go on with your daddy
An' have a lot of fun."

In town, Pa walked us over
To the small movie theater,
An' said "I'll go an' do my chores
An' pick you two up later."
When he came back to get us,
We stopped to have some snacks,
An' eagerly we checked out
All the contents of his sacks.

I told Pa about the movie we'd seen,
Indignation in my heart,
As I told him of the action
In the most exciting part:
"These three rustlers stopped the lady.
They were terribly impolite.
When the cowboy called them on it,
They started this big fight.
They were throwin' fists an' punchin'
An' rollin' all around,
An' then those cattle rustlers
Had that cowboy on the ground.
Well, that gal just stood there watchin'
With a look of pure dismay,

An' I'll be darned if then
She didn't faint just dead away!"

"Well, if that cowboy needed help,
He couldn't depend upon her,
With those odds of 3 to 1,
I thought that cowboy was a goner.
If I'd been there, I'd a jumped right in
And fought to help my man!
I'd have grabbed aholt an' bashed those guys
With a shovel or a pan!
Papa, I don't understand
How women are portrayed.
Why are all the cowboys' ladies
Always weak and so afraid?"

With eyebrow raised, he turned to me,
A strange look in his eye.
If I live to be 100,
I'll remember his reply:

"Women weak? Now, Honey,
That sure makes me laugh!
The things you see in movies
Don't tell the truth by half.
You can't always see her courage
In the way that she'll behave,
But it's hard to beat a woman
When it comes to bein' brave!"

"Now your Ma's a good example
Of the women in the West.
If I had to have just one ranch hand,
I would pick her from the rest.
Your Mama can ride with the best of men,

An' she throws a mean lassoo,
She can drive a team of horses
An' she's helped with brandin' too!"

"She's a dead-eye shot when she has to be,
Remember that rattlesnake?
Now, don't you go to thinkin'
All she does is clean an' bake!
No man I know is half as brave
In puttin' up with pain;
She'll work longer hours than the men
An' never will complain.
If someone tried to hurt you kids,
She'd tear them right apart,
If she's not ridin' bulls an' broncs,
It's cause she's too danged smart!
You never measure courage
By a willingness to fight.
It takes far more strength to live your life
Doin' what you know is right!"

Back at home, I helped Mom put away
The things that she had canned,
An' I looked at her with clearer eyes.
Pa had helped me understand,
That I could be a ranch hand
Or a mother or a wife.
There are many different ways
To show your courage in this life!

Grandma

I remember my old grandma
In visions sharp and clear.
I can hear her, I can see her face
As if she were still here.
She was a feisty lady,
A working rancher's wife,
And you could tell by looking
That she'd had no easy life.

Though her wrinkles showed
The years she'd lived,
A girl's twinkle was in her smile,
And she'd waltz me round her kitchen
In an energetic style.
She had married my grandad
When she was just sixteen,
And stayed right by his side
When times were good,
And times were lean.

Through six children, sons and daughters,
To which she joyfully gave birth,
Through the heartbreak that they faced
Returning two sons to the earth.
Side by side, they stood together;
Through the years they both did toil.
They were aged oak trees sheltering us,
Roots firmly in the soil.

And Grandma's was the heart and hand
That kept us all together.
She gumptioned up the meek of us;
The wild ones, she'd tether.
And when she dished out treats,
She saw that each one got his part,
But she always saved the biggest piece
For Grandpa, her sweetheart.
As she patted Grandpa's head
Or bent to kiss him on the cheek,
More love passed between those two
Than words could ever speak.
I can see her figure standing
By her old wood-burning stove,
Or stepping spryly up
Into the pickup truck she drove.

My grandma gave me honest talk
And the wisdom of her years.
My grandma gave me cookies
As she wiped away my tears.
My grandma gave me spunk an' grit
To make it through each test,
But it's the love that Grandma gave
That I remember best!

Lessons Tooled in Leather

Like fine-tanned leather, our lives are molded
And stitched firmly into place,
And so my life was molded
By the tools from my grampa's case.
It was after school and on holidays,
When our classes were adjourned
That I'd listen to his quiet voice
And life's greatest lessons learned.

My grampa was a saddlemaker
Outside our country town.
For the quality of the things he made,
I knew he was renown.
And his quaint and crowded workroom
Was my favorite place to stop.
How I loved the smell of leather and wood
That filled the tiny shop!
I would help him check the skins for flaws,
And I'd put his tools in order,
And every day he handed me
At least one shiny quarter.
And I'd help him case the leather,
And I'm sure my eyes would shine
As I watched his rough hands
Delicately tool a fine design.

If my chattering questions bothered him,
He gave no indication.
I'd watch him shape the saddle tree

With the greatest fascination.
I remember the answer that he gave
When I asked in childish prattle,
"Grampa, why does it take so long
To make a single saddle?"
He answered, "A cowboy buys a saddle
That'll last him most of his life.
If you think about it that way,
It's sort of like picking a wife.
It's got to be nice to look at;
It's got to have staying power.
It's got be something comfortable
For many a working hour.
As time goes on,
Though it might get worn
And maybe need repair,
A quality saddle is something
That gets better with the wear.
And some like their saddles fancy,
And some like their saddles plain,
But everyone knows that the saddle's made right,
If the saddle bears my name."

I'd watch him put the finishing touches,
With which he spared no pain,
And see the pride in his finished work
As he stamped it with his name.
I'd enter the saddle number and date
Into the log he kept,
And I'd pick up the leather bits and scraps
As around the shop he swept.

In warm weather, we'd sit outside
And drink a soda pop,
And folks would honk and wave
As they drove by my grampa's shop.
In wintertime,
Before his old pot-belly stove we'd sit,
And have a cup of cocoa
When it was time to quit.

Then I started making reins and halters,
Latigos, and straps,
And Grampa let me practice
Leather toolin' on the scraps.
I moved up to making larger pieces
As my skill increased.
I took to braiding rawhide,
Creativity released.

When I finished my first saddle,
Everybody came,
And Grampa gave me a new small stamp
To etch it with my name.
I said, "Grampa, I will cherish this,
But on one thing I'm resigned:
I'd like to keep <u>your</u> name stamp on my work,
If you don't mind."

And my Grampa is long gone now,
But to this day you'll see
His name still stamped on all I make,
A sign of quality.
He left me his little workshop.

He left me all of his tools.
But more important, he gave to me
A set of guiding rules.
And he gave to me a working code
Which I am proud to claim:
"Everyone knows that the saddle's made right,
If the saddle bears my name!"

Growing Up On A Ranch

Growing up on a ranch was an experience that was at once rich and limiting, knowing and innocent, busy and contemplative. Children grew up working with the cowboys from the time they were old enough to sit a horse. They knew about nature and weather and mating and birthing. They were unsophisticated in city ways. Long on manners, they were taught to respect the land and their elders. They had a freedom to roam that most city children never knew. Many everyday chores were performed by the children and accepted as a way of life. Everyone had to pitch in to provide the necessities for life on a ranch. Families were closely knit, and neighbors were people you could depend upon, whether you liked them or not.

An' How I'd Ride

I never will forget
The very first time that I saw it,
There I was a-walkin' down the street.
We had come in to the general store
To pick a few things up,
An' Pa gave me a nickel to buy some sweets.
As I moseyed to the ice cream parlor
To buy some penny candy,
Somethin' in Joe's window caught my eye,
The prettiest saddle I'd ever seen
Was sittin' on a stand,
I can't describe its beauty, but I'll try:
It was smooth an' shiny-lookin',
Not too fancy nor too plain,
With a little leather toolin' on back an' side,
An' I knew that if I just
Could put that saddle on my horse,
Gosh, Almighty, I would have the finest ride!

An' I'd ride out on the desert,
Out amongst the sage an' brush,
An' I'd feel the joy of bein' young an' free,
An' I'd chase them ole jackrabbits
'Roun' the sand hills with mesquite,
An' I would be so happy to be me!
-- An' how I'd ride!

When I went into the store
Just so's I could touch the saddle,
There was lovin' admiration in my eyes!
An' Mrs. Joe, she came right up and said,
"Why don't you try it?
I do believe it's just about your size!"
An' my, but it felt fine
When I climbed into that seat.
I said, "Thank you kindly, Ma'm, for lettin' me try it.
I hope that saddle doesn't sell,
Cause I'm gonna save my nickels
An' when I've got enough, I'll come an' buy it!"
An' I ran to tell my pa about it,
But he just looked sad
An' stood there with his hands down at his side,
"Now, don't you git yer heart set,"
But he didn't understand,
If I only had that saddle, how I'd ride!

An' I'd ride up in the mountains
Over thin an' rocky trails,
An' I'd look out as far as you can see,
An' even hawks would envy me
As they flew all about,
An' I would know the joy of bein' me!
-- An' how I'd ride!

Throughout that year I kept that saddle
Foremost in my mind,
I saved my nickels, though they were mighty few.
I worked hard for my pa

An' even went to nearby ranches
To ask if there were chores that I could do.
When we would go to town,
I'd go into the saddle shop,
An' spend as much time there as Pa'd allow.
Mrs. Joe would let me polish up
The saddle with a cloth
An' she'd ask, "How much do you have saved up now?"
But then one day we went to town
An' the saddle had been sold,
An' I can't tell you just how much I cried.
My hopes had all been scattered
Like gold dust in the wind,
No longer could I dream of how I'd ride!

How I'd ride among the canyons
With their shadows cool an' long,
Explore each crevice with the greatest glee,
An' my laughter would scare out coyotes
Hidin' in the caves,
Because I'd be so full of bein' me!
--An' how I'd ride!

For a month or so, I moped around
Like my heart had clean been broken,
No coyotes howl would have been as sad as mine.
But my pa kept me a-workin'
An' he made me ride my horse,
It was spring and gettin' close to calfin' time.

Ma also kept me busy
Doing chores around the house,
Cleaning out the barn an' oiling up the tack.
Then the mornin' of my birthday dawned,
An' my folks led me outside
To my horse with that special saddle on his back.
How I yipped n' hooted n' hollered,
An' I even hugged my pa,
An' when I kissed my ma, she up an' cried.
Then I jumped upon my horse
An' like a bullet we shot off
To take that long-awaited, magic ride.

**As we rode off towards the desert
'N the canyons 'n the hills,
Every livin' thing that watched could clearly see,
Like a dust-devil a-growin',
Too strong to be contained,
I was full of life an' happy to be me!
An' I'd never lose the joy of ridin' free!
--An' how I'd ride!**

The Old Schoolhouse

The building stands deserted now,
No sign of life I see,
Just an ordinary-looking house
Beneath a great, old tree.
The sight of children playing out front
Is seen no more;
There are no students running
Through the one-room schoolhouse door.
As I approach, I almost think
My teacher's voice I hear.
My hand wipes dust from window pane;
Inside the room I peer.
And Time decides to play with me,
As it does now and then,
The years go speeding backwards,
I'm a child once again.
My vision blurs, then sharply clears,
I'm held as in a spell.
I turn to see my teacher
Walk out and ring the bell.
From out of nowhere, students come,
They seem almost to explode.
My brother, late as usual,
Runs down the curved, dirt road.
Inside, we sit at tables
Eager youngsters, set to learn.
Since all grades are in one classroom,
We must calmly wait our turn.

Pencils move across paper;
Chalk moves across the board,
The teacher moves from chair to chair,
No child is ignored!
The morning passes quickly,
The clock's hands do reveal:
It's time to send the children home
To eat their noonday meal.
And I skip out of the building
Into the blinding sun,
As the time-warp seems to shatter
And the magic is undone!

I turn and see the schoolhouse,
Sadly empty, weather-worn,
I have witnessed in that room
My thirst for knowledge being born.
The importance of the things we learned
I now appreciate.
We learned patience, diligence, respect,
How to cooperate.

And I think, "If there were some way
For every child to do it,
I'd have them experience a country school,
Education as I knew it!"

Cowboy Lullaby

I remember as if yesterday
The song my ma would sing,
An' the words to it, I find, can soothe me still.
She would softly sing it to us
As she'd rock us in her chair,
When we were feelin' sad or feelin' ill.
An' that chair was carved by granpa.
He was so proud he would say,
"The best I ever made, an' I'm not braggin'.
I made it for your granma
Right before your ma was born,
An' we brought it out here in a covered wagon!"
My mama's voice was sweet an' clear.
It filled the small ranch house.
I shore caint sing, so I won't even try,
But I want to save the words she sang,
So they won't be forgotten,
To the tune she called "A Cowboy's Lullaby" :

Hush, my little baby, there's no need for you to fear,
Your mama's gonna hold you, oh so tight!
There is nothin's gonna hurt you, so you needn't be afraid
Of those noises that you're hearin' in the night.

**Safe an' sound, safe an' sound,
On the ranch or in the town,
God's babies all are sleepin' safe an' sound!**

Those are coyotes howlin' out a celebration of the dark,
If you listen, that's a strangely pretty tune,
Cause those coyotes are so happy to be out there in those hills
That they're singin' to the stars an' to the moon.

Safe an' sound, safe an' sound,
In their dens or on the ground,
God's babies all are sleepin' safe an' sound!

An' that hootin' that you're hearin' is the callin' of an owl
Tellin' everyone that it is time to rest,
That it's time for little children to be tucked inside their beds,
An' it's time for chicks to be inside their nests.

Safe an' sound, safe an' sound,
In the roosts or on the ground,
God's babies all are sleepin' safe an' sound!

An' the whistlin' you're hearin' is the night herd out on guard.
He is singin' to the cattle as he rides,
Cause, like children, cows are skittish,
An' they tend to be afraid
Of the noise they're hearin' in the dark outside.

Safe an' sound, safe an' sound,
On the range or homeward bound,
God's babies all are sleepin' safe an' sound!

Safe an' sound, safe an' sound,
On the ranch or in the town,
God's babies all are sleepin' safe an' sound!

Cowboys and Love

There was not a lot of time for courtship in the cowboy's life. Perhaps the most romantic thing about him was his independence, his love for the outdoors, the vitality he derived from his outdoor, active lifestyle. These things made him attractive. Cowboys tended to be cavalier in their treatment of women. They either stayed and settled or they moved on, breaking hearts...not much different from the emotions we experience today, but perhaps less complicated. In the final analysis, cowboys were and are men, and cowgirls were and are women, with all the human sentiments and passions natural to each.

The Dude Boots

Now I'll have to go back to the beginning,
Where this story has its roots,
So you'll understand the moral
About this pair of boots.
Being a true Texas girl,
I grew up riding horses,
But I had to leave the ranching life
Due to determinate forces
(Such as having to earn a living
And needing money, as a rule)
And I found myself in the city,
Where I worked and I went to school.

After a few years of living
Around pavement and machines,
I gave away my old riding boots
And my worn-soft, working jeans.
And several years went by
Where I had no chance to ride.
Though I must have looked like a city girl,
I was a cowgirl deep inside.
And being a true Texas girl,
Some things still brought me joy,
Like two-steppin', an' the rodeo,
An' a good-looking cowboy.

And on some quiet weekends,
'Stead of staying home to mope,
I'd drive out to the valley,
Where the cowboys'd come to rope.
It was there on a Friday night,
As we watched the men compete,
That a smiling cowboy came along
And swept me off my feet!
He was interested in me,
Of that there was no doubt,
And I hoped before the evening ended
That he would ask me out.

Sure enough, he came and asked,
"Say, can you ride a horse?"
And being a true Texas girl,
I answered, "Why, of course!"
"Would you like to ride tomorrow?"
I answered, "That sounds great!"
He said, "See you in the morning.
Don't forget, we have a date!"
In the morning, my mind shrieked,
I have no time to prepare!
It's been years since I went riding!
I've no proper clothes to wear!

Morning found me putting on jeans
That for riding were a trifle tight
And I pulled on the only boots I had,
Which for dancing were just right.

They were short and soft-skinned leather
With a gold band on the toe.
As I looked into the mirror,
I almost hoped he wouldn't show.
But, of course, he was quite punctual,
And how my heart despaired,
When he asked, "Are you all set to go?"
And at my boots he stared.

Well, we got out to the horses,
And I could see that he
Was going to ride this flashy horse,
And he'd picked a nag for me.
Being a true Texas girl,
I checked out the horses there.
As I picked a pretty spirited one, said,
"I want to ride that mare!"
"Naw," he condescended,
"I don't think she suits.
Why don't you ride this other one?"
And he looked down at my boots.

"Now I told you, I'm a Texas girl,
And I know how to ride."
Reluctantly he went into the corral
And brought the mare outside.
He saddled her up for me,
And I can still recount,
Between my tight jeans and my nervousness,
I made a wobbly mount.

And he said to me, "Now normally,
I'm not one who disputes,
But are you sure you want to ride that horse?"
He glanced quickly at my boots.
For answer then, I kicked my horse
And "hyaa" I shouted clear,
And we shot out for the open land
With him bringing up the rear.
I could hear him yelling from behind
As the wind whisked through my hair,
And I figured, with his attitude,
He deserved a little scare.
I knew he thought I was out of control
As we flew over the ground,
So being a true Texas girl,
I circled my horse around.

We came up at his side;
then we left him behind.
I thought, *This will teach that cowboy
To keep an open mind!*
We went around some sand hills
And over a little ditch,
And then my feisty little mare
Began to jump and pitch.
For half a minute (though it seemed longer),
I rode her as she hopped;
Then it seems that she'd had enough,
And I brought her to a stop.

I looked over to where the cowboy watched,
Admiration in his eyes,
And he smiled a grin as he said to me,
"Girl, you've been a big surprise!"
Now being a true Texas girl,
I said something quite astute,
"Don't be so quick to judge someone
By the style of their boot!"
And he admitted what he had learned,
Though I thought that it would kill him:
"It's not in the kind of boots you wear,
But the way in which you fill 'em!"

A Cowboy's Love

Now, listen to me, Ladies,
If courtship's on your mind,
When it comes to pickin' cowboys,
Beware of what you'll find!
He'll make you fall in love with him
If you give him half a chance,
But there are certain cowboys
That don't know much 'bout romance.
They're used to ridin' all alone
And not sayin' very much,
An' most of their communicatin's
Done through just a touch.
They're most comfortable praisin' you
The way they would their horse,
And my last cowboy boyfriend
Told me this, without remorse:

"I'll never understand
Just what you ladies want from men.
Just when I think I've figgered it out,
I find I'm wrong agin!
It'd sure be nice if when
Your ladyfriend broke into tears,
You just could reach right over
And scratch her 'tween the ears.
An' if you could give her a carrot er two,
An' she'd whinny a lovin' call,
An' if when you didn't want her 'round,
You could put her in a stall,

An' when she was especially good,
You'd give her a sugar lump
An' show her that you really cared
By pattin' her on the rump.
It'd be nice if women'd be satisfied
With a single set of shoes,
An' you could rein them in
Just like a runaway cayuse.
If you didn' have to call 'em up
An' ask 'em for a date,
An' you could tie 'em to a hitchin' post
An' they would patiently wait.
If women weren't so squeamish
'Bout rollin' in the dirt,
An' you could come a-callin'
Without wearin' a clean shirt.
I guess you could say my horse an' I,
We have an understandin',
An' I sure wish that womenfolk
Could be so undemandin'!"

Well, needless to say,
That cowboy an' I didn't make it very far.
He rode away on his stallion;
I drove away in my car.
So before you pick a cowboy, Ladies,
Just as a matter of course,
Be sure that you check out the way
That cowboy treats his horse!

The A,B,C's of Cowboys

A friend of mine once said
In great sincerity, no doubt,
"Honey, I've become a pro
At checkin' cowboys out!"
So I listened while she explained
As clearly as you please,
That cowboys could be separated
Into groups of "**B**'s":

The younger cowboy lives a life
That keeps him very active,
And many factors do combine
To make him so attractive:
His body's lean an' wiry,
Strong-shouldered, muscled arms,
An' a trim an' tapered waist
Is an addition to his charms!
His skin is tanned a golden bronze
From workin' in the sun,
Which accentuates the smile
That he flashes you in fun.
He wears a western shirt
That's tucked neatly in his jeans,
An' he proudly shows a buckle
That he's polished till it gleams!
His trim an' hardened body
Shows a molded derriere,
Shown off by fitted blue jeans
As he swaggers on his way.

So in pickin "**B**'s" to summarize young cowboys:
They're the ones,
That could best be categorized
By their **b**uckles an' their **b**uns!
Now, your older cowboy, generally,
Is one who's gotten wise.
He tries to leave the active work
To all the younger guys.
His body's lost that tautness,
Now the tautness is in his jeans,
As he appears to settle
Into sedentary routines.
His skin that once was golden bronze
Now has turned to leather,
From workin' outside all those years
In every type of weather.
He's used to eatin' hearty meals,
An' these he'll still consume,
But because he's not so active,
His stomach starts to bloom.
He doesn't shine his belt buckle
So as not to call attention
To the fact that round his middle,
He's increasin' in dimension!
An' soon that buckle cain't be seen,
It will almost disappear
Underneath a saggin' belly
That gets larger every year!
So the label fer this cowboy,
Though it's one that he disputes,
Is the one that categorizes him
With two "**B**'s": **b**ellies an' **b**oots!

But whether he is young er old,
Thin or heavy too,
One thing about a cowboy,
He's a gentleman, through an' through!
An' he never lets a chance go by
To start a friendly rumor,
That'll make some people laugh,
An' show off his sense of humor.
Within every cowboy's chest,
Beats a heart that's young an' free,
An' "**Blessed**" with love of freedom,
That's the cowboy's greatest "**B**!"

On the Trail

Life on the trail was a set of paradoxes. It was at once busy and boring. It was the camaraderie of the cowboys and the loneliness for those left behind. It was the excitement of new towns and the monotony of everyday work. It was a freedom of soul and spirit enwrapped in the strict rules of work and behavior on the trail. It was days and days of nothing new, and then moments of tense danger. And it is this image that the world would capture and hold, of the cowboy as he rode his horse down the trail.

Roundup Time

They were sandy an' gritty an' dirt in your eye,
An' the cattle kicked up so much dust,
You scarce could see the sky.
They were ridin' an' ropin' an' wranglin' all day,
An' stretchin' yourself thin
For not an extra dollar's pay.
They were bettin' an' badgerin' an' boastin' all aroun',
An' lots of talk bout what we'd do
When we got into town.
They were heifers an' dogies an' longhorns to chase,
An' pushin' your poor pony
To near neck-breakin' pace.

For the roundups were a man's world
Never meant for faint of heart.
In that world of reckless courage,
Cowboys played the biggest part.

They were biscuits an' gravy an' coffee strong as pitch,
An' eating Cookie's stew
That we nicknamed "Son of a Bitch."
They were jokin' an' singin' an' stories roun' the fire,
An' contests to establish
Who could be the biggest liar.
They were aches an' groans an' grumblin'
As we rolled into our beds,
An' the stiffness in the mornin'
When our bodies felt like lead.

They were rules an' codes an' rituals
That the ramrod did enforce,
An' close communication
Between cowboy an' his horse.

For the roundups were a man's world
Filled with work an' fun an' strife,
An' the cowboy thrived upon it;
Herdin' cattle was his life.

For the roundups were a man's world,
An' most everyone would say,
That the roundups were the best part
Of life the cowboy way!

Line - Camp Christmas

So many nights I spent alone
While ridin' on the line,
But it never bothered me quite so much
As it did at Christmas time.
I don't know why I felt that void
Since I had no family
With which to spend the holiday
And gather round a tree.
Wherever I was ridin' herd
Was the place that I called home,
An' the gear that I had with me
Was all I called my own.
My wintertime companions were
The horses in the herd,
An occasional coyote, And a solitary bird.

At the camp was a mongrel dog
That I had taken in,
And she, along with my ole horse Gabe,
Made up my closest kin.
But being lonely that Christmas,
I cut down a little pine,
An' I took some tops of tin cans
And attached them with some twine,
An' on Christmas Eve I gave ole Gabe
An extra flake of hay,
An' settled Dog right next to him
To sleep till Christmas Day.

On Christmas morn, I woke right up
And got a fire goin'
An' looked out of the window
To see that it was snowin'.

I bundled up, an' quickly,
I gathered gear an' saddle.
I wanted to get an early start
At checkin' on the cattle.
But when I got out to the shed,
Dog didn't welcome me,
And Gabe was just a-standin' there
As quiet as can be.
I walked inside to check things out
An' foun' to my surprise,
Lyin' next to Dog were three small pups
With tight-shut eyes.
Dog lifted up her head to me
An' slowly licked my hand,
An' I knew this was a Christmas gift,
Though she wouldn't understand.

An' though that other stable
Was in distance an' time so far,
I thought I'd name the puppies
Gaspar, Melchior, an' Balthazar.
So the spirit of the season came
In a manner vast an' strange
To this lonely cowboy an' his horse
Spendin' Christmas on the range!

CHUCKWAGON CHARLEY

You will read about the heroes
Of those famous cattle trails,
Of the wranglers
In the spaces wide and free,
And you'll read about the cowboys
And their days upon the range,
But you'll never read
A word of praise 'bout me.
Fer I never rode no bronc
Ner dressed in spurs and Stetson hat,
And that is why
I always get the snub,
But I was most important
To those long, hard cattle drives
Cause I'm Charley,
The man who cooks the grub.

I was the first man to be awake,
To get the fire going,
And the last man
To finish work at night.
When it comes to feedin' hungry men,
The cooking's never done.
You need lots of food,
And you better fix it right!
Cookin', bakin', fryin', boilin',
Mixin', gratin', stirrin', mashin',
Choppin', peelin'

Wore my fingers to the nub,
But their clean plates said they liked it,
And every now and then,
One of them would say,
"Thanks, Charley, fer the grub!"

So I never will be famous
In the annals of the West
Ner a member
Of the cowboy heroes' club,
But no cavalry or roundup
Could have traveled very far
Without Charley,
The man who cooks the grub!

Mail

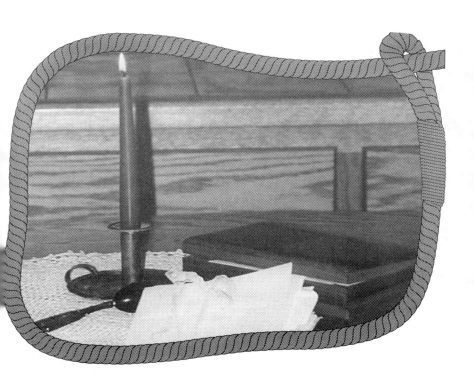

It was difficult to keep track of loved ones in the West once they moved away. Mail delivery was sporadic. People waited months, even years, for those few precious lines scratched out on bits of paper by candlelight, fireplace, and campfire--for it was in the evening that people had time to be lonely and think of their far-away loved ones. Letters were read and reread, till paper crumpled and yellowed, and were saved with locks of hair, to be treasured.

Lock of Hair

The fire cast its flickering light
Into the cold night air,
Illuminating the stretched-out forms
Of cowboys sleeping there.
At a distance, the night hawk
Was singing a slow tune,
And the cattle moved like shadowed ghosts
Beneath a clouded moon.
One cowboy sat with paper,
And leaning to catch the light,
Licked pencil tip so slightly,
As he began to write:

"My Dearest Girl,
It seems so long
Since last I saw your face.
We are moving with the cattle
At a brisk and steady pace,
And each day takes us further,
And each day without fail,
I think of you as we move down
This long and dusty trail.
I think about your smiling eyes,
Your face that is so fair,
And... have I ever told you
Just how much I love your hair?

And the lilt of your laughter that follows me after
Makes me feel like I'm dancing on air.
How I love the sunlight on your hair!

The days are so long; the nights are so cold;
The blazing sun is so hot.
We've met with no big misfortunes,
And we pray that we will not.
I hope this letter reaches you.
There is so much that I would say,
But my road leads to Montana,
And you're so far away.
In my mind, I see you reading this
In your front porch rocking chair,
And, by the way, have I told you...
How much I love your hair!

And the tears in your eyes as we said our goodbyes
Fill my sad heart with despair.
How I wish I could touch your soft hair!"

As she read his words, the young girl
Struggled not to fall apart,
But the thoughts within that letter
Filled her hands and filled her heart.
And she pictured her young cowboy
Sitting on his dapple gray,
And the look that he had given her
Before he rode away.
Then she stared up at the mirror,
At the girl reflected there,
And smiled at what he'd written,
"Do you know how I love your hair?"

And the memory stayed like a song that's been played;
She would whisper it like a small prayer,
"Have I told you how I love your hair?"

Like a river flowing one way,
Sometimes we can't turn back.
The cowboy never made it home;
He died in a line-camp shack.
They didn't know who to write to;
There was no one to notify.
While they put up a small wooden marker,
There was nobody there to cry.
When they went through his belongings,
They could find but little there,
Just some worn and yellowed letters
And a lock of golden hair.

And the young cowboy lay in the sandstone and clay,
And they placed on his breast with great care
The much-treasured lock of gold hair.

As the years went trickling slowly,
The young girl would wonder why
The cowboy never returned to her,
And her letters got no reply.
Though she went ahead and lived her life,
She never forgot the cowboy,
When she was feeling lonely or low,
One thought brought her comforting joy:
As she'd sit before her mirror,
Her brush would pause in midair,

And she'd whisper oh so softly,
"How he loved my shiny hair!"

As her hair turned to gray, you could still hear say
As she sat in her porch rocking chair,
"Now have I ever told you
How he loved my beautiful hair?"

And she knew in her heart that they never would part,
In heaven, a lifetime they'd share,
And she'd always have long, golden hair.
How he loved her beautiful hair!

Mail-order Memories

"He's coming! I can see the dust
Of his truck headed our way!"
It was Tuesday at the ranch,
And it was mail delivery day!
Mr. Buddy drove his pickup truck
Along the bumpy road
With letters, cards, and parcels
As his much-awaited load.
And we'd hop into his truck to see
Which boxes had our name,
But the thing that we liked most was
When our mail-order catalogs came.
We'd fight over who got first choice
Of those things for which we'd yearn,
Till Ma sent us to bed early,
Just so's she could have her turn.

There were things in there for everyone!
There were toys an' tools an' tack,
And it said in great big letters,
"IF YOU DON'T LIKE IT, SEND IT BACK!"
They couldn't make it easier;
It was there for all to read.
We could order anything we saw.
"SATISFACTION GUARANTEED!"
Though some of the things for which we asked
Would fall upon deaf ears,
We got many wondrous packages
Throughout our growing years!
My mama ordered seeds and plants.

She even got some trees!
Gramps got this funny safety suit
When he started keeping bees.
Mack always ordered Western shirts
With genuine pearl snaps,
And one year for his birthday
Got some fancy leather chaps.
My sister and I, when we were young,
Seems like we wanted toys,
But that changed to clothes an' beauty stuff
When we discovered boys.

From farrier tools to liniment,
Horse shoes to sportin' gear,
Our Christmas gifts and birthdays
From those pages did appear,
And more joyful than receiving them
Was the thrill as we'd peruse
The pages with their pictures
To see what we would choose.

It is something I remember,
Even though the years have flown:
Our Santa drove a pickup truck
And let us shop at home.
I still love to look at catalogs,
Though it isn't quite the same
As those days we waited on the ranch --
When the mail-order catalogs came!

Horses

The image is imbedded in all our minds: the horse runs freely over the open ground, neck stretched forward, mane flowing into the wind, tail held high and streaming backward like an aileron. This is the spirit of the cowboy personified: strength, power, agility, surefootedness, free-spirited, the unwillingness to be enclosed, tied down, or tamed. It was the horse that created the cowboy...that gave him his mobility and his nobility. The bond between a cowboy and his horse, even though he rode many, was special. Whatever they went through on the trail, they faced together. Horses were and are a great equalizer. When on horseback, a man, woman or child, young or old, large or small can keep pace with each other. Like Pegasus, they give us wings, and allow us for even a few moments to feel almost like gods.

My Best Pal

Some cowboys need no possessions;
They're always movin' on.
They'll ride for you three seasons,
An' the next one, they'll be gone.
So I never collected objects;
Few clothes, my gun, my tack,
No more than I could roll right up
An' place at saddle back.
It never bothered me that
I had nothin' of my own.
I settled into believin'
I would go my way alone.

But then, one day, I rode into
The town of Abilene,
An' there for sale was the prettiest
Paint horse I had ever seen!
So I went right to the trader,
An' without excess palaver,
Negotiated a deal, because
I knew I had to have her.

I gave the man my cash, my horse,
My gun an' holster too,
An' a 14-karat buckle I'd won
For "All-around Buckaroo."
As I led that horse away with me,
Somethin' made me feel,

That she was really worth it,
I had gotten the best deal!
So I found a ranchin' job
That would keep us both in feed,
An' we settled down to workin' hard,
Me an' my trusty steed.
She had the sweetest disposition
Of any horse I'd found,
She seemed to take right to me
An' just followed me around.

When we were workin' cattle,
She'd anticipate each need,
An' do anythin' I asked of her
With agility an' speed.
She was great fer pleasure-ridin'
At a smooth an' easy lope,
But she'd really come down hard
On those cattle we would rope.

There were cowboys tried to buy her
Many an' many a time,
But I never gave it a second thought,
This wondrous horse was mine!
She was more than just a work-mate,
She was good fer my morale,
She was all the fun I had in life,
My confidante, my pal!

We covered the West together,
For more years than a score.
I rode my pretty paint horse

Till she could ride no more.
Then I settled down in one place,
The greenest I could find,
An' I turned her out, for I wouldn't leave
My trusty friend behind.

Life's filled with such sad endings,
But this much I will allow,
I had a Paint, a horse, a pal,
My God, I miss her now!

Wild Horses

They carried us Westward o'er mountains and sand.
They pulled covered wagons and helped plow our land.
They charged into battle with valor and speed
And on farms and ranches filled many a need.
Now tractors and trailers have taken their place,
And on modern highways, the autos do race.
Because on their use we no longer rely,
Out on the range, wild horses do die.

With loads on their backs, over uncharted trails,
They carried the scouts and transported mail.
Pulling caisson and cannon and overland stage,
Left indelible marks upon History's page.
Now they're a luxury we can't afford,
And the government won't pay the tab for their board.
As we watch in frustration with tears in our eyes,
Of starvation and thirst, the wild horse dies.

What a sorrow it is that this fate should befall
The most beautiful, noblest creature of all.
Technology's failed if it can allow
The horrible injustice that's happening now.
No running or prancing with tail held high,
But staggering weakly, the wild horses die.
On terrain over which their hooves once went flying,
In scorn and betrayal, wild horses are dying.

Cowboy Code

There was an unwritten code, adhered to by most of the cowboys, which governed their dress, behavior, manners, work ethics, and values. Some of it was certainly learned from the older cowhands with which the young boys worked; some of it derived from the stringent rules set by the ramrod on the ranch, and the discipline required to get the cattle moved to market over the rough trails. The value codes perhaps stemmed from the fact that those drawn to cowboying were of the same mind in the style of life they desired. Many of these codes remain unchanged for the modern cowboy. External factors have changed, but expectations of cowboy demeanor have not.

Code of the Cowboy

My father was a rancher and a cowboy through an' through,
A strong man who could bear most any load,
And he showed us through example
What was right an' what was wrong,
And he lived his life by what he called "the code."

It was a code of conduct and of being fair an' square
In treating every creature in this land,
And if we kids forgot it, as we all did now an' then,
He'd remind us with a firm, but loving hand.

"A man's word is a promise never broken," he would say.
"In life, we harvest just what we have sowed."
"Be honest in your dealin's, in all you say an' do."
These things were elemental to the code!

"You always lend a helpin' hand to someone that's in need.
Treat all women like they're ladies. And, of course,
If somethin' evil threatens you or anyone you love,
Do what you have to and experience no remorse!"

"There's no use in complaining 'bout things you can't control.
If you don't like it, then just hit the road.
Don't take yourself too seriously; laugh at your mistakes!"
These too were basic values of the code.

Pa taught us, "Never pick a fight, but never run away!
Be sure to pay back any debt that's owed.
A cowboy's not a bully, but he stands for his beliefs,
An' he runs his life according to the code!"

We kids would tease about it, as we were growin' up,
But we made sure that our laughter never showed.
It took us years to understand how lucky we all were
That Pa had raised us by his cowboy code.

One thing we all agree upon today,
Is that we will raise our kids the cowboy way.
For of all the gifts with which we were bestowed,
The greatest was to learn Pa's Cowboy Code!

A Cowboy's Thanks

What's a cowboy thankful for?
There's not much he does need!
He's not one for collectin' things;
No trace in him of greed!

The things that mean the most to him,
Nature does provide,
And some loved ones there to share it with,
Working by his side!

He is thankful for the rain that falls
And turns the grass to green,
For the water that is pumped up
By the windmill, fresh an' clean,

For the breeze that blows
And cooly dries the sweat upon his face.
He is thankful workin' out of doors
And keepin' up the pace!

He appreciates his rough voice
Raised in song or hymns of praise,
And the friends who gather round
In time of need and holidays!

For the fireplace sending out its warmth,
For the dinner on the table,
For the stock a-lowin' in the night,
For the horses in the stable!

And he's glad that in this lifetime
He's experienced this elation -
The awe-inspiring feeling
Being part of God's creation!

For cowboys are aware
Of all the changes on this earth,
And appreciate the miracles
That come from death and birth!

And he's thankful there are still
Some open spaces clear an' wide,
Where a cowboy can get on his horse,
And he is free to ride!

The Changing West

The face of the West has been changed by technology, by a westward-expanding population, and by environmentalists, fences, and government rules and restrictions. Some of these changes have made the cowboy's job easier; most of these changes have threatened the cowboy's existence. But ranch people have responded to them with the same courage and tough determination to hold onto a way of life that their forefathers displayed. If people everywhere are fascinated with the cowboy, it is because they recognize something worthwhile and desirable when they see it.

Entrepeneur

My daddy was old fashioned
In the things that he believed
And we knew he was fair minded,
Though he often had us peeved,
Cause he'd assign each one of us
Some chores we couldn't shirk.
His motto was, "If you live here,
Then you help to do the work!"

And I did the same as I raised my kids,
But I found to my frustration
That it's not so easy dealing
With this modern generation.
Now my oldest son was in FFA;
He was always a succeeder.
One day he said, "You know,
I joined a club for business leaders,
And I have to form a business,
Get something I can sell.
I'll have to make up market plans
And develop a clientele."

The next thing that he said to me
Was a real flabbergaster,
"I guess I'll be too busy, Mom,
To be cleaning up the pasture."
I jumped right in and quickly said,
"Oh no, you won't, Senor.
Around this house, we all pitch in

And help to do the chores.
As it happens, you're the oldest,
So the stalls you have to muck,
And I'll expect to see you
In the pasture with the truck."

He pouted just a little,
But the next day I did see
He was shoveling in the pasture,
As busy as can be,
And he asked me, "Do you mind, Mom,
If I work for other neighbors?"
And he smiled when I queried,
"Are you selling manual labor?"

With his younger brother and a friend,
He formed a business team
And painted on the truck,
"Turn your lawn and gardens green."
Now I'll tell you, one month later,
Did I feel like a dumb bunny
When my son showed up with a prize he'd won
And a whole fistful of money.
And I'll admit, I really had
To admire this young man
As he told me all the details
Of his winning business plan.

"You see, Mom,
    Country folks have a high respect
For a young man with ambition,

So I called on all the people 'round
And made them a proposition.
I'd clean their pastures, stables, stalls
For a fair amount of pay,
And for a few bucks extra,
I'd haul it all away.
Then I drive the loaded truck to town
Where all the folks are sure
No fertilizer's quite as good
As organic, clean manure.

So we sell it by the truckload,
And we have found that they
Are glad to have us spread it
For not too much extra pay.
They can pay us to run the mower
And crush it up real fine.
They can even pay us to water it in,
If they are so inclined.
And the best part of the business
With which everyone's impressed
Is that I can get my product
Without having to invest.
And our neighbors gave me contracts,
Their business to assure.
By gosh! I think that I have cornered
The market in manure!"

"Well, Son, I thought you'd be
A cowboy like your dad,
But if you stay in business,
It might not be too bad.

And I think you've given recycling
A whole new connotation!
Why, the horses and the cattle
Will pay for your education!
But somehow I feel that people
Don't relate 'entrepeneur'
With a young man who is out there
Shoveling manure.
And somehow I believe that
Unless things really change,
Your product will never be featured
On the commodity exchange!"

Why?

The lonely sailor looks out at the vast expanse of sea
And he looks up at the stars that fill the sky.
As he watches whales cresting, lovely creatures dancing free,
He can't help but ask the angry question, "Why?"

And the lonely cowboy looks out at the vast expanse of land
As he watches cattle slowly drifting by.
He sees the world a-changin' and he doesn't understand.
There's an anger in him as he utters, "Why?"

"Why is it that the people who live closest to the earth
Have no say in trying to conserve it,
While the men who make the rules
And determine grazing's worth
Look at dollar signs in trying to preserve it?"

And the senators in the East say, "Raise the grazing prices!"
And Japan buys Haiti's vote on whaling rights,
They certainly don't care what the rancher sacrifices
Nor of the whale's death throes as it fights!

And they ship out all their sludge
To dump upon the open ranges,
Bury radioactive waste beneath the ground.
They think it's all just empty land, spaces void and barren;
Don't bother them when dying cattle are found!

And a family that's ranched the land
For at least three generations
Is told to cut their cattle herd to half,
And authorities seem unaware, or maybe they don't care
That by this, they're writing ranching's epitaph.

Yes, they'll save the great horned owl
And the tiny spotted trout,
While they let the cowboy slowly disappear.
But then cowboys can't contribute much
To political campaigns,
And - it always seems to be election year.

So they order their thick steaks,
Charge them to expense accounts,
Then run to cast their vote on the next treaty;
While the common person can't afford
The rising price of beef and thinks,
"Boy, those ranchers sure are getting greedy!"

And the rancher sees his grazing rights
Grow smaller and more costly,
Gets a limit for his herd he can't defy
From a man who'll never mount a horse,
Nor drive a herd of cattle.
Who will cast his votes and never bat an eye.

And the rancher is not deigned with a reply
When he asks the sharply pointed question, **"Why?"**

THE GOOD OLE DAYS

In the good ole days....
    Men were men and women were women
    And you knew the rules for treating each in turn.
    And menfolk weren't found working in the kitchen.
    It was the woman's job to milk and mend and churn.
Nowadays....
    Folks all dress alike,
    And two wage families are the going trend.
    The sexes are clamoring "Equal treatment!"
    And I wonder where it's ever going to end.

> **Oh, I miss the days of roundups,**
> **Herding cattle on the range.**
> **Life was hard, but so much simpler.**
> **I find the new ways strange.**

In the good ole days....
    The cowboys rode out each day on horseback,
    Riding fences, working with the cattle.
    In heat and cold, dust and grit we traveled.
    We'd spend the whole day sitting in the saddle.
Nowadays....
    The cowboy's steed has a five-speed transmission;
    He takes his truck on trails where weeds have grown.
    In a heated, air-conditioned cab with tape deck,
    The real cowboy's world is one he's never known.

How I miss those days of roundups
  There is nothing I'd exchange
  For the memories of my horse and me
  Riding lonely on the range.

In the good ole days....
  The chuck cook always hustled up the best food.
  There was nothing ole Charlie couldn't do
  With big, black cast-iron pots over coals or fire,
  He'd cook a feast for a tired, hungry crew.

  And everything smelled and tasted better
  When cooked and eaten in the great outdoors,
  And there wasn't a one of us big cowpokes
  Who didn't ask if we could have some more.

Nowadays....
  Well, I hear that outdoor cooking's gotten popular
  And that everybody does it in these parts.
  And experts have gone and made it easy
  By writing up these recipes and charts!

You know....
  Chow still tastes so much better
  When cooked outdoors on the range,
  And I'm glad to see that in this life
  Some good things never change!

End of the Trail

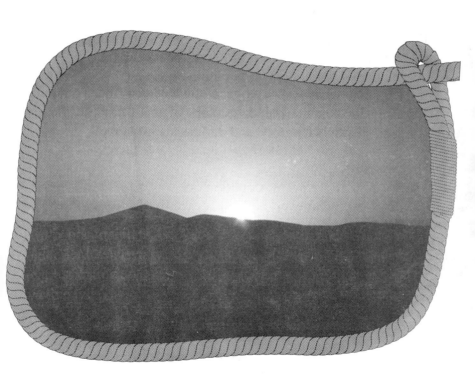

For each day there is a sunset, a time to recognize the end of the working day. It is a time of peace and beauty--and acceptance of the brevity of our hours in the sunlight. We can reflect upon what we have accomplished, and cast one last lingering look at the blended colors of the skies and of our lives, as shadows lengthen and darkness approaches.

Sunset

The day was coming to a close
As I rode out on the rim.
It was getting close to sunset
And the light was growing dim.
My horse knew where I'd want to stop.
He was used to this routine.
This was the best spot on the mesa
From which to view the scene.
It was one I never tired of.
I had seen it grow and change
From the day when I had first arrived
As a young man to this range.
Back then, there had been nothing
Across the valley floor,
Grass and brush, a few trees,
And very little more.
To have these acres as my own,
I'd gone into huge debt,
And over the years I'd paid for it
In time and tears and sweat.
With our hands we built our first house,
Ran fences, water lines,
Invested in good breeding lines
For livestock of all kinds.
We made it through the hard times,
The years of heat and drought,
And I'm thankful that my children
Never had to do without.

We never made much money,
But I didn't ask for wealth.
We were rich in things that mattered --
Friendship, family, love, and health.
And I have few regrets
About the life that I have led,
But my greatest fear is ending life
In a strange nursing home bed.
I sure hate to admit it --
I'm not the man I used to be.
Though I've fought hard to outrun it,
Age is catching up with me.
I just don't have the stamina.
I try not to complain,
But arthritis and old broken bones
Are causing me some pain.
And my kids try not to notice,
But it's hard to ignore:
It takes me twice as long to saddle up
As it did before.
They pretend that they don't see it,
Or they look the other way,
Cause getting on my horse
Is getting harder every day.
An' if they try to help me,
I get ornery and mad,
Though if I were to be honest,
What I really am is sad.
If I could do the planning,
When I knew the end was near,
I'd mount my horse and ride away,
And we'd just disappear.

But I've children and grandkids who worry,
And they think they know what's best,
So one of these days, they'll take the reins
And put me out to rest.
But listen, faithful pony,
Until that day appears,
I'll ride you to this lookout spot,
Just like I've done for years.
And I won't think of dying
As leaving a life that's dear,
But that this old cowboy is riding off
To explore a new frontier.

Treasure

My daddy once told me, "When all's said and done,
You'll never get rich a-cowboyin', Son!"
He was just being honest; that was his belief,
And he figured that maybe he'd save me some grief.
Once he'd been a cowboy, but he'd left that life
Cause he couldn't provide for his kids and his wife.
But I knew that he missed it. I'd see in his eye
That flicker of longing as I would ride by.
And I said to him, "Daddy, some might call me fool,
But I've found in my lifestyle a treasure of jewels.
I've collected these gems from each place that I've been,
And in my own mind, I'm the richest of men.
I've sapphire garnered from heavens of blue
Though I've seen them look turquoise and vary in hue,
And I rode fields of lapis that made my heart sing
When the bluebonnets bloomed down in Texas in spring.
I've had nights of black onyx that later gave way
To opals as sunrise stretched out to grasp day.
The world fills with diamonds when the weather does freeze
And the ice droplets shimmer on branches of trees.
And the amethyst beauty is hard to surpass,
When in springtime, the blossoms of sage do amass.
The new-budding leaves are a peridot green
And the wildflowers the yellow of sunny citrine.
I've emerald pine trees and fields full of jade
In the growing alfalfa and coarse grassy blade,

And rubies and garnets that bring such delight
Streaked across heaven as sun drops from sight.
I'm a rich man in fortune I never will spend,
For the treasures of Nature go on without end,
And in cowboying, Daddy, I've found me a place
That is simple and natural and filled with God's grace.

Immortality

We live on earth for but one brief moment --
A blink of an eye in the history of time .
And short the days of youth and free abandon
And swift the days when we are in our prime.
But within that span, we reach out for the world
To imbed our fingerprints upon its face.
Hungrily we grasp at all the passions,
Seizing love and laughter at a breakneck pace.
Through each failure and success we do accomplish,
We discover who we are and what we'd be,
And then we're gone, leaving just a trace behind us;
Branding one small corner of infinity
With the energy and vitality of our being,
We have burned our mark on the eternal scroll.
We have etched one letter on its endless record,
And stamped it with the imprint of our soul.
Though the trail the world will follow is uncertain,
We have helped the great Head Wrangler lead its way,
As our past stampedes into the great tomorrow,
What matters is the life we live today!